RISE
Andrea Perry

Guelph, Ontario

Written by Andrea Perry
© All rights reserved

Cover image by Sue Crawford
© All rights reserved

ISBN: (pbk) 978-1-928171-27-0
ISBN: (ebk) 978-1-928171-28-7

Vocamus Press
130 Dublin Street North
Guelph, Ontario
N1H 4N4

www.vocamus.net

For my Family.

ACKNOWLEDGMENTS

Many thanks to master poet, Kevin Connolly, for opening the world of poetry to me and for setting such a fabulous example of person and poet.

Great love and thanks to forever friend, Sue Crawford, for sharing her Heart and Art for the cover of the book. Sa sekhem sahu.

Deep gratitude to Jeremy Luke Hill of Vocamus Press, without whom this book would not exist.

"Lost in Sonoma" was inspired by a lyric from the song "Multitude of Casualties" by The Hold Steady.

"Designated Knowledge" was previously published online by Vocamus Press.

The titles of the poems "Triumphant Success", "Accelerated Motion", and "Rejoice in Celebration" were taken from a deck of tarot cards.

The figure of "The Master" that appears in several poems is inspired by Lao Tzu's *Tao Te Ching*, translated by John H. MacDonald.

RISE
Andrea Perry

It's totally counter-evolutionary:

We fucked off the entire earth

& brought ourselves to the brink

of extinction.

Only now

we are re-membering.

"It is not a reversal of trajectory, but a rise."

PREFACE

Before you begin,

      There   is   a   code

        in   this   poem

        to   upgrade

        your

        DNA

    Read it three times

    and up side
        down

  and   the   rest   will   fall

        into

                                                place
                                                peace

HUMAN APPOINTMENT

"*the Universe only cracks when its individual parts cease to perform their designated function.*"

~ So be yourself

   Will you?

You were born that way, as they say, on the radio   but don't take my word for it which is *s i n c e r i t y* of thought and form   listen   to the contract printed on your fingerlips   it's at the base of the brain   in your instinct compartment which takes orders from the   vascular   cavity   which dips into the galactic reflex   and all spawned in a wicked red pot of broiling   stardust
It's been pre-arranged with no stipulation
that any or all of it should be followed

But I'd rather live as a shoe
with a tongue
than a cast iron fire place
made of bamboo
burning itself out

1
THE BEGINNING

COVERT BRILLIANCE

People are less like apes
more like fireflies
carrying a secret pocket of light
in our bellies

One must only know it is there
to ignite
the fields of density

DESIGNATED KNOWLEDGE

When they guessed what was near, they buried it fast, used their hands,
tools of timber and rolled stone. They raked up paths, sprinkled it in silt.
Pried open hilltops, packed it in. Sunk it to river beds, set it in sludge.
Peeled the fields back, and laid it tenderly beneath the civilization to come.
An extraordinary secret in plain under sight, under foot but hardly felt,
barely heard, unless one spread himself out and put an ear to the pulsing earth.
After they passed, only the trees knew, drew it up and splintered it skyward
to signal the rest.

They buried it fast but buried it shallow,
just under the lid of the world, hopeful we wouldn't be too long noticing.

IT IS NIGHT AND SOMEWHERE

beyond the tracks, a fragrant ash splits the earth.
Bellows from her spring to summon the passengers
shunting by life in thousands, cloaked in woolen coats.

The train has stopped for no apparent reason to teach us
a lesson in waiting. We look out the windows and see
nothing of use. A tree is still in the black wind.

Through the cart's open door, I cross the wide plain
up a knotted trunk, sit nimble among many boughs.
Crouched in bloom, I travel home.

LOST IN SONOMA

Though we know it's a valley,
the Sonoma seems high
as hell on something.
Trees are radiant and wacked out.
Dogs scratch, shivering and smashed
peeling up sidewalks.

We know it's a valley…

We spend a few months
just wandering, trying to find our way
out of the haze
but nothing's familiar,
cept for the multitude of corpses
swimming in sewers
shoulder bones seeping out
of man holes.

We know it's a valley, it's a valley…

We grow to love it,
forget it isn't
what it should have been.
Can't recognize a thing
other than those sodden fingers
prodding through drain pipes
into our baths.

It's a valley, it's a valley…

Even our insides are sleazy,
off somehow,
like the Sonoma's invaded
our blood stream, come in
through the belly button and spread
her things. There's an imposter
hunched in our eye sockets
scissoring our retinas.
But he looks so good
in reverse.

Something, somewhere, still knows it's a valley…

The Sonoma's crammed its arteries
with our discarded selves,
pumped us through its veins.
We shine out
the streetlights in panic.
But, this is home now.

Don't lose it, doesn't look it…

We should lay out, rest awhile,
but it's been so long
the only thing we're aware of now
are the bodies under the streets
our friends.

ONCE UPON AGAIN

Brushed your elbow at Shopper's Drug Mart
saw us covered in red dust, polishing stones
into spades

Let you gas up my mid-sized sedan
the way you worked the pump reminded me of those tedious defensive stands
on the ramparts

Stood behind you in line for the premiere
your hands punched into my armpits to drag me off
the Somme

Kicked you out of my classroom
couldn't help but wonder, why you'd picked me?

Kissed you
imagined my hands around your neck in a hayfield

Followed you into the crapper
knew we'd done this before, somewhere

Let you hitch a ride
and bobbed side by side like we were back
 on the Oregon

Heard you drop a toonie into my coffee cup
remembered how you'd stopped for me when no one else would

Texted you by accident
the way you typed *Must be the wrong John* was like a lightning bolt
                                                              to my third eye

Took a picture of you at the zoo
recalled how I had once borrowed your coat to cross the tundra

Commented on your Twitter feed
didn't realize how much I owe you

Rubbed my pelvis, discreetly, against your backside at the club
which only felt like the first time

Let you make a left turn, though I was at the stop sign first
and just knew you'd taken advantage of me before

Saw you on a billboard with a milk mustache
figured, at some point, you must have been my mother

Rescued you from the Humane Society
to make up for that time I'd left you
behind

Operated on your open heart
recognized those creases
in your lips

Brought you your order
felt you pulling at my ligaments

Knocked noggins going for a greeting card
and was overwhelmed
by the most tremendous empathy

Proposed to you
even though you'd said no for centuries

Pressed your spangled wings into a crack in the sidewalk
with my boot

Shived you in an alleyway
and reminded myself to thank you for saving my life
so many times before

PARTICULAR IMPACT

Atoms sling off my head
in your direction

Vibrations paddle the air
between us

My fingertips strafe you
with tidings

The space among us disintegrates
under a microscope

Though we've never met, we're all standing
in the wretched heat, waiting for the same bus

This submolecular communion is deft
So I'm careful to hit you, strangers, with love

THE CREATION GAME

Threw them out of the galaxy, as far as they would fire, BANG-BANG, an empty casing, a feck among specks craning back into black matter. Who's got bets on who to remember first? Which lonesome creature will turn its gaze inward, open an ear, and find us talking, gambling on the artists or the quarterbacks, the clerics or the vagrants, mothers or fathers? Angel's eye observation on an elastic-man stretched to infinity, recoiling back on itself before the SNAP, fall-out.

The view is spectacular
seats are wide
but how long might this go on?

Who will return alone,
and who will come bearing
all the rest?

STAR-SEED ANCESTORS

The pyramids were built from space
that much is obvious.
And the way the stones were arranged
in Mazatlan, Stonehenge, and that other island
I can't remember.

Such precision, a giant hand must have descended
from the heavens and drawn them out
with a pointed instrument – the one
in the little plastic geometry case –
I can't remember.

The hand was feathered, though,
that's for certain. Stellar blue,
with scales on the wrist
and a lion's mane for a bracelet.
The fingers were tails, could be a dolphin's
or a whale's, either or.
All of them are up there, looking down –
they can't remember
whether we were worth it or not.

So they keep plucking us up by our heads
and putting us down elsewhere,
prying our eyes open
with an enormous elephant's tusk.

NUMEROLOGY

Twos.

                        Eleven eleven 11:11
                        four   four   four
                         4   4   4
                            5   5   5
                              777
                               8
                       8   9   10
               eight eight eight eight eight
                        11,12,13

                                                                          Sixes.

It's midnight under a blood-moon
and the drowsy man's soul
listly considers the mathematical probability
he'll heed its bearing, sometime
this lifetime.

He reclines on the evening blankets,
running equations with a finger
tracing the constellations
like a streak of rubber on the pavement
after a car accident.

He dozes. Returns.
According to the Indiglo, it's 3:33.

RE-DIRECTION

Dropped my toothbrush under the grey edge
of the bathroom counter.
Took a minute to pick it clean of cat hair
and other specimens
I refused to eye too closely

so missed my bus
and got fired
from a job I hated anyways.

Got a new job
fearing lack of funds and mis-understanding
the requirement to be someone,
but on the first morning my shirt got stuck
in that forsaken space
at the center of the washing machine

by the time I pried it loose
not only was I late, but had a sizeable rip
at the seam of the shoulder
that my boss spotted with a tilted eye
almost immediately.

No longer my boss, no longer employed,
I keep looking for jobs on the Internet
but the power goes out
for no perceptible reason
every time I click 'submit.'

Switched over to dating sites
thinking a relationship will do
if I can't find a job to fill that forsaken space
at the center of my chest
I noticed just yesterday in the mirror.

Must have been there for some time.
It is shockingly large.

Lots of options on the sites,
however, whenever I make plans
to meet up with a girl
something happens

like that time my phone died
or the ragged stranger harassed me on the street
way-laying just long enough
so I could see the back of my date's soft head –
which looked lovely – bending into a taxi.

I am tired of these obstructions
and the hole in my chest has grown itchy,
beginning to show signs of malaise,
red spots
that I tried to pop with tweezers
but the tweezers broke in half.
Explain that?

I've been prodding it
for hours. This hole feels ungodly,
only it *is* a holy hole
that's the point.

It doesn't need to be filled
simply opened further
and aired out, that would cure it
I'm sure.

A bit of sunshine, perhaps
to soothe the split rim.

Unfortunately,
nobody told me that
so I keep looking for jobs
and people to love
but can't stop dropping things
or tripping on cords
which leaves me un-plugged for days

with nothing to do but return to the mirror
and examine my chest
pondering the re-directions.

DARNELL BARTON, BUFFALO METRO

Saw 'er hangin' loose off the guardrail
over the I98. Back to the bar,
chest fallen out forty feet
above traffic
rollin' on below.
Head clearly thinkin' there was no reason
not to drop in front
of that semi.

People strolled past 'er with a half look,
half step that almost halted,
and carried on by.
So stopped my bus, called it in,
got out, offered a hand,
which she took, surprised
that anyone had noticed
or cared.

CREMATORY

Arrived on my table
with a ring 'round your neck.
Beleaguered design of the willing
I'd seen twice before.

So I tended you carefully,
buttoned to the chin,
boots double-knotted,
kissed your soles, sent them onward.

And when you passed through
the cathedral's ancient flue
as a caravan of black smoke

you dispersed wholly
into the unspoilt sky.

INTERVIEW WITH THE MASTER

Welcome for coming! (hands her a black mic bud)

I'm wearing a dress, not a lapel. You'll have to put that somewhere else, kindly

(furniture is re-arranged around a circular table with a vase-jar, petals mattressing
                                                                                         on filmy water)

Let's pitch the camera down, Richard . . . why don't you start by telling us what sort of shoes you've anchored in?

My feet are bare. Anyone in plain sight can see that

(removes and washes spectacles. A spritz from under-side curtain left)

It's the eye, not the lens that must be clear

I see where this is going

(folds hands in lap)

Let's get down to it. We're all up here and nowhere else, aren't we?

What would you like to know?

Speak about the refugees, bleeding out the Middle East, tainting our drinking water
    not to mention our social services, and our children, who are just kids, let's remember

(looks firm, yet open) It's a decision point

You'll have to get more to the tip

A trajectory of choice between Love or Fear (slides forward) . . . did your ear collect the capital letters?

The specificity has been recorded . . . right, Richard? . . . and what are the consequences regarding humanity's decision on this matter?

Simply a New World or the Old World . . . did you—?

Yes, we got it. And I suppose this new world is love? Correction: Love

One and the same

What about all these see-saw elections? Seems rather tumultuous

A choice

Let me guess

Fear or Love

I see (removes and replaces spectacles)

Do you? It's a tremendous opportunity. We have been waiting a long time
                                        waiting (checks watch)

Would that 'we' have been capitalized if it weren't at the head of the sentence?

Yes

And what constitutes this 'We?'

All of us

Even them?

Yes. It must be everybody or nobody

And how might this unity be possible?

Inter-web of consciousness

Correction, stand by . . . did you mean to say, Internet?

That, too

Do we . . . pardon . . . do 'We' need everybody to get everybody?

Of course not   (points to the overhead lights, saucering)
Critical mass is the central requirement

So you're telling me the shift is exponential?

As you mentioned, a see-saw. There is a point at which the balance transitions

But a see-saw can go back, up and down, left and right

Not this time

So it is only up, once the leverage is passed?

I believe you already know the answers to these questions

But since you're here in the present flesh, I'd like to take advantage . . . tell me about the increasing energy of Earth, statistics are staggering

Imagine a fever, to burn off what damages the Host

So you're telling me this is advantageous and not a catastrophe?

It is what we have all been waiting for and it will be very gentle

But you said (reviews record) 'burn off,' which to me implies pain

The pain is up to leave. I suggest you do not hold on to it and, as I said, it will be very gentle . . . the winds of change

(flowers stir in the vase on the table, a miniscule movement)

There. Did you feel it?

PLAN IN ACTION

Sat together side by side, on the moon,
just at the end, on the smooth round of the crescent,
warm as midnight milk, hand in hand
our feet swinging in tune
to a galactic heartbeat, our four shoes
playing, drawing star-streams across
the marshmallow anti-matter of the Universe.
From below, someone might have thought the streak
some strange plane's tail of exhaust
or an unknown constellation, strung out, flickering.
We loved this view of earth
on down days with nothing to do.
But that night, it was all business: A plan must be made.
The world was not well and the prayers drifted daily
to our ancestral ears, pleading for intervention.

We said we'd meet at a party, you 29
planning suicide by 30, and me one year behind.
(How I loved you as an infant, by the way, your downy
blond head and curious eyes, even at three months I swear
I saw them look up, carried from the car, to catch me waving,
stamping the night with a secret sign, anxious to come down).
The party would be un-scheduled till the last minute –
serendipitous. You, fresh from the tattoo parlour
with a double-breasted wolf on your upper-arm, in the city
for a week-long trip. And me, sent to the area for school,
ready to abandon love
and take the task alone.
We had one mutual friend, Allison: 'The Linchpin,'
who had gone two years prior to set things up.

"I think you'll like my friend Amanda," she said,
running the lines we had given her
before she descended with the vanguard
on a night-ship of crystal rain.

We would know each other at first sight,
or so we thought.
But bodies don't look so familiar in three-dimensions.
Unexpectedly dense, loaded with gravity and memories
from 29 years we had now spent apart, no longer shared.
The light that used to pulse from the skin now hidden,
deep within the eyes. Yours brown, still curious
but dreaming more frequently of a noose, or a razor
to the wrist; mine blue, in colour and in mood,
because I couldn't figure out how I could be so *lonely*
surrounded by everyone but you for nearly three decades.

No conscious recognition
standing across from you in the kitchen, spilling wine
at your socked feet, but somewhere inside our thick bodies
a button was pressed.
We had coffee and went home, you back to the East Coast,
me to class, where, as I listened to a lecture on the narrative
possibilities of poetry, I felt something growing in the vicinity
of my belly button – an invisible cord – drawing me away
from my desk through a wormhole of dimensions
to your doorstep, where I watched you put on your shoes
and unlock your bicycle from the fence. I waved and hollered,
but you didn't see me, walked right through me, in fact.
In shimmering disarray I heard your sad, singular thought:
'What is there to live for?'

Had some idea now, who we were
and why we had come.
But I couldn't just call you up and say, "Hey, listen!
Remember that time on the moon?" So I played it cool,
keeping in touch at a distance, a smiley on your status,
a Facebook message here or there, a text, in the evening
where you would admit you had been thinking about me
when you were trying fervently to think of anything else *but* me.
And every day I felt the cord turn thicker, winding itself
on itself, pulling us closer, stomach to stomach.
You were provinces away but I was sure, could we see
our other-worldly reflections, we would have been sandwiched
belly to belly in a small crevice, cozy under rainbow lantern light
on the back-side of the moon.

When you hurt, I hurt.
When I cried, I noticed the pink puffs under your eyes
on Instagram, unmistakable evidence of a torturous night
spent just the same as mine. Your pain was confusion,
a spiralling energy reminding you how far you had fallen
from where we were. Yet you couldn't place it.
My pain was a hopeless, distant view of the one you love
struggling against themselves, asking to be *anywhere*,
anyone else. And though I reached
and I reached, it seemed
that the plan we had made was flawed.
We had given each other too much,
and when you heard my voice in your ear at night,
the weight of my absent head on your shoulder,
you brushed it away, feeling nothing but the awful sensation
of being so close, yet so far, from what you seek.

Or is this just part of the whole calculation?
And after I write this poem and send it out,
you will find it one day in your local library
on the back shelf. In some anthology, with hundreds of pages
but only this one dog-eared by the previous reader
to catch your attention.
A precious, hand-picked reader with coloured lights
in her fairy eyes.
One of the vanguard
shipped ahead, so long ago.

MOONSHINE

I was hungry, but when I learned it was a mistake
to eat, I turned this crescent belly in degrees
toward a veiled sun, and saw that it was full.

Oh yeah!

I crooned 'em, the shrunken houses
scattered across stretched wet plains below.
I slid through cool windows, lit softly on their noses

and when they came up from their beds
in the morning, they were happy,
though they did not know why.

SLEEPER CELLS

He woke belly down in a field of cattails, still dark,
stripped the wet bits of reed from his shirt,
split a section of stalk to peer ahead, and located his friend
on the edge of the marsh with his head down

under a willow tree, canopy of angel hair, dome of slumber.
Tapped the friend on the shoulder with a loose branch,
woke with a start and started off down the rear path,
bared feet imprinting, to the end, where a tent had been erected

triangulated over two sleeping bodies. Shook their night bags
and up they went in opposite directions: One to the train tracks,
one to the abandoned smoke-house, where at both locations
somebody lay snoring under a section of cardboard

once rattled, they rose and went on through the lightening darkness:
One up a water tower where the city could be seen as stars
on a bullet-point map; one up a hilltop electrical apparatus,
mechanical titan over-watch. And on each, others had fallen asleep

along ledges, propped against metal poles, limbs dangling, over-hung
in the cool breeze, drizzle of drool stretching to earth, some orange
sliver on the horizon. Once roused, they climbed down, dispersed as spokes
over the landscape. One into a creek bed, one behind the treeline

and others toward town, along the pale streets, into the back
of a bar, the waiting room of the doctor's office, the middle row
of a movie theatre, where everyone had nodded off. Shaken, in seconds
they found more: Behind the pulpit, in the confessional booth

head like a stone on a bible, at the podium,
knees locked, swaying on foot, behind the news desk
in front of the camera, zees going out on wireless wave
to living rooms and satellite radio, group viewings

and personal phones. Even to the government establishment,
where papers stuck to wet cheeks. Prodded,
they all rubbed their eyes and stared out the windows
at the rising light, and up they went to search out others.

Bodies turned up on dented couches, dusty beds, in classrooms,
rooftops and storage cellars, under the stock shelves,
manikin ticket-takers, flash-frozen cashiers, behind the wheel
of aircraft. And with each one woken, the party grew

moving together now in coordinated effort. A Procession,
and as it passed, the trees danced, grass stood taller
in relief. A cheer from the gardens, around the town
and under foot, insects raised a thousand happy fists

mammals skipped in their furs, the birds
conducted a fly past in recognition.
There was one uncovered in a back alley
who couldn't be wakened. They poked him with a broomstick,

shouted in an ear, lifted a shoe.
Someone tickled an eyebrow with a feather,
pinched the loose skin behind the knee
called his name mildly, until they could wait no longer

and departed into daylight.
And though nothing had moved on the surface,
inside the sleeper a mitochondrial cell buzzed and opened
its lids, brushing its neighbour to signal the morning alarm.

ROMANCING THE SUN

They met at a party. The sun was in the corner by the TV
blazing back a second Somersby Cider. She was in a flash
in an instant, sidling over with a hand above her peeking brow,

"Are you a woman or a man?" she asked. "Both," said the sun.
"That's hot," she sweated. The folks on the sofa lifted some shades
to cover their eyes and went on talking like they weren't listening.

"What were you first?" she asked. "I was always everything,"
the sun shrugged, rolled its orbs, melted the can in its hand
and reached for another.

Someone under the hanging portrait removed their shawl
and fished in an elephant purse for tanning slaw.
"Are you happy?" she squinted, "I can't quite make you out."

"Yes and no," the sun tugged at its perimeter,
"I'm not always comfortable in my skein, plus I burn all my clothes,"
it raised an eye to itself, "so it goes."

She paused, offered the thought, "Perhaps you're trying to be something
you're not?" "Not that I know of," said the sun, removing its shoes
and depositing the ash in the rubbish bin.

She watched, admiring the streaks from its chin, the rays of hair
all over its body, a lightness, the unmistakeable inner glow, equal halves
masculine and feminine, severed straight through the middle

where there was no divide.
She cocked a hot head: "I think I might love you immediately.
Is that silly?" Something flared on the sun's surface – a jolt

through the inter-space between them. "Not at all," it said,
opening at the center in an endless grin.
"I'm glad you mentioned it first. We've loved each other since

the beginning, only we're just meeting now.
I would have been hurt if you didn't recognize me."
Two hearts sizzled,

twin flames.

"Smells like hamburgers in here," someone leaned into the room
and left for the kitchen. Another turned a fan on overhead,
which only drew the temperature higher, scorching the ceiling.

The sun and the woman regarded each other through matched eyes,
"This must be why it never worked with anyone else," they said
in unison, laughing at the symmetry. Unable to escape

the fractal effect, all the partygoers giggled too, brightening in their seats
and stands. "Can I take you out for coffee tomorrow?" she asked.
It was late, the clock on the wall read 11:30 post-meridiem, pre-midnight,

and everyone was now in swimming suits with silver placards
under their faces, reflecting. The sun whirled 'round to face her
from the other direction: "I'm not a morning person," it shrunk,

filled back out, "mornings disgruntle me. Can you deal?"
She was open-faced, eyes white, stringing in the light,
"How is that so?" "So it is," said the sun.

"Couldn't you just stop coming up if you don't like it?"
The room straightened, held a damp, collective ear to the situation
in the corner. "Well that would be no good for anyone," the sun sighed

a momentary volcano.
"You seem quite self-less," she said.
"I have no self," the sun grew, receded,

"And I don't discriminate who I shine on,
even when I'm raging!" There was a shock, the TV buzzed
and went out, the music stopped.

The room roasted in silence.
The sun lowered itself, shame-faced, dipped below the horizon
of the coffee table: "I always interfere with electricals."

"I don't mind," she stepped closer, nose and lips blistering.
A puss and a pop, an ooze, a slop. The sun rotated to the long end
of the table for distance, dropped a couple solar flares

to the shellacked surface, weeping: "I knew it.
No one can handle me. I'm too powerful, unpredictable.
I know you're the one, and it still can't be done."

The voice was muffled under the table. Everything inside
and around the room rumbled, even out on the streets, the whole world
appeared to split and retreat, run off down the block, waving

a purple flag.
"It isn't true," she said, coming around, her hair singed at the tips.
A hand out to comfort the broiling ball, she touched the fire

and screamed!
– a moment to adjust to the influx –
then stilled, at peace.

"See?"

The sun peeped. It rose, wary. "You're still here?"
"I feel better than ever," she beamed, super-charged with heat.
A joint release of grief by the guests smoked to dissipate.

"And now we're all better off," she said, watching the snake of smoke
leave through the open window. "How is it possible?" asked the sun, rising further.
She gazed down at her red hand, de-particalized

constructed of nothing but sunlight.
The hand drifted to each side of the room, spreading,
grazing cheeks and foreheads, breast holes and back bones,

disseminating the love she had for the lost sun.
"We're made of the same materials,"
she said

and as the sun recalled, so too did every guest
in attendance burst from their skins to populate
the party with seventeen returned stars.

2
INTERMISSION

"We are the ones we've been waiting for."

THE RISE

*The rise of humankind
has been calculated for centuries
upon millennia*

*It was only the fact that
we didn't know
it was up
to us*

*So we waited, begging
the saints
the stars
the books
for divine assistance*

*un-aware
they were already helping
they were already here
they were us
all along*

THE RISE 2

The rise of human-kind
is not an ascension
of some

But a re-membrance of One
and a harmony
of all

A snow-covered pasture rounding
the breast of the earth

beyond sight

white pelt
knit with seven billion snowflakes
none the same

                                  connected, geometric matrix
                                  all in hand

                                                        crystalline

3
THE BEGINNING

THROAT CHAKRA

They lined the babies on the bridge and forked them
into the broiling water, Pacific pot of steaming skin and soup
and mothers screaming on the black shoreline, looking at you
with a communal accusatory eye, because you said
nothing.

They bricked ovens large enough to accommodate millions
of unwanted persons,
bodies burning, disintegrated: they came out the frozen flue
and streamed through your nostrils
to smoke up the inside of your skull, and lay a soft knock
on that paralyzed part of your brain
that was meant to identify gross
wrong-doing.

It would have been better, had you said something.

The city was half underwater, a spiritual paradise,
a science-based race, equal parts intelligence and heart
or so they claimed. But you knew better, and watched it all go down,
slipping into an ancient scorpion sea, now mythologized,
but you *still* know better.
So you better say something
Others fantasize, yet you can see it clearly in your mind's eye,
bright as the day it sank, sun-tipped golden rooftops dipping below
the shattered surface of the water, dragging the dreams of the Universe
to settle with the lilting algae at the bottom. Dank, lost, forgotten.

So you better say something, for God's sake.
For the sake of God, at least *write* something.
Disguise it in a poem if you have to,
somewhere between the lines and the metaphors
a simile of truth.

He's touching your breasts now, and you thought you said no,
but you can't be sure because your voice is so small,
the reed in the flute of your throat seems to be strained
from a failure to adequately exercise the muscle for so long.
Over thousands of incarnations, it has hardened to a pit,
seized up like an Adam's apple on an Eve.

He's un-doing your pants with lizard fingers, but if you can
just get something out, for God's sake,
get something out! A scream or a shout will do.
Speak! You will redeem yourself

and in the same collapsed breath, transmute the awful lifetimes
of silent horrors erstwhile.

THE OTHER

Cattle stood uddered in the pasture
bleating into the shrill
darkness.
Something was barrelling down
from the hills,
coming for us all.

So I strode through the damp night
to touch its shining forehead.

NON-JUDGEMENT

Being, as it was, near the base of a stone hill
rare sun found the sallow tree.
It grew listlessly, bent crudely east,
slackened in bare soil.

Still finches paraded untroubled along its tangled spine
and when they came from the hall in the afternoon
the men did not think what a rotten, rotten tree.

SOURCE VIEW: A MICROCOSM OF THE MACROCOSM

The Earthworm

Most of you step on us because
you think it's funny how we carry on
as two.

But one
notices the rain is done, the sun has come out
and lifts us from the sidewalk
before we burn.

The Rock

You like to skip us in rivers
and pick us from the soles
of your shoes

and don't seem to appreciate
the stain we leave on your hands
from our time here.

But some do
place us on the altar
of a dresser.

The Spider

'That thing is from the fucking crypt,'
It's not like we don't know
that's what you're thinking.

Only *she* lays on the dock
peering through the slats at our webs
suspended over the lake

whispering
with a heart in her eye
"I see you."

The Mouse

We must state our case:
the cats are unwanted.
So if you could be bothered to come out
and remove our bodies from their playful jaws,
we might leave you something
in a stocking, or at the back of a drawer
under your t-shirt
that you have been asking for.

The Pinecone

If you feed us to the dog, it's okay.
We can feel the excitement, too,
spreading over the park in pieces
as water-droplets on a desert.

The Ladybug

I landed on your shoulder for a reason
to speak in your ear the answers
to the questions you shouted from your bed
last night.

I won't use words, but listen
to the twitch of my spotted wing
sending Morse Code
to your nervous center.

If you flick me off
you have only yourself
to blame.

Though we understand, of course
that your senses may be impaired,
strained under lifetimes
of silt.

Hair

You dropped me in Mexico,
behind the hotel toilet. And one in France,
on Juno Beach, that has since been stepped
into the depressed sand.

You left me floating on the Rhine, one in the crevice
at the bottom of the Berlin Wall, and several
all over Moscow, in Lenin's Tomb
on the Red Square, under a tourist's walking shoe.

A couple here and there in a village
by Lake Victoria
where there was a genocide.
And another south-west on Copa Cabana,
washed into the Atlantic
on the crest of the tide.
All pre-placed, so that when you awakened
your DNA made a map of the world
lit up like that children's toy – Lite Brite –
that you used to play with,
not by coincidence.

The Eagle and the Wolf

I am a lonely eagle
if you observe nothing but my majesty
far over-head.

Like the wolf
skulking in the winter evergreens
separated by shadows.

Placed apart
because fear and love
are opposite sides of the same coin
and it is physically impossible
to have more than one
face up.

THE RED ONES, ATHENA AND SON

There's a chin-up bar in the bedroom door and books
tossed all over the desk: Wisdom and War

"Athena's a bitch" he says dropping his text
and shapeshifting 'cross the hall   She sees

a cougar   compact   He's lighter on four feet
Erect he stomps past the television displacing his power

into the floorboards 'cause there's nowhere to put it
in the classroom or in the workforce beyond he can see

nothing that interests him   "You were just something else"
she says "Did you notice?"

"Nope!" His steps sound up the stairs
like he's rising to Olympus: "I'm bored"

In a red suit and red dress it's more obvious
there's something about them

They're not from here   It's in the eyes
Her colours passed on to him   He straightens

his bowtie: "I feel like myself in this outfit
for some reason" It's the only thing he's worn

that doesn't bulge at the seams with his frequency
emitting haphazardly she raises a question to re-direct it:

"How have the others in your grade been treating women?"
"Not well" he says   He will be different   "And their parents?"

Not well   He will be different and she will be too
"They pissed all over the school bus"

Power mis-laid   She lifts her antennae to dissipate
the frustration

chakra sonar pulse to the stratosphere
and back

The lights flicker out all over the house
"What the fuck? My Game"   He's playing

League of Legends   She leans over his shoulder
stale grilled cheese plate for days and points to the stalled

screen: "Those are all you" she says   A dragon
constructed of birch bark   a butterfly

with chemical compounds
an elf with an over-sized heart

He's smaller than the others his age but she's not concerned
their packages were chosen to best effect

And when he feels her radiating in front of him he can't reconcile
what he reads in his text book

"I can see through other people's eyes" he tells her
for the first time and two provinces over

the father receives a shock
and settles in to Themself   surprised

"Will we have to fight?" the son calls down the hallway
head on his pillow   skipping dimensions

There's a cat in each room
unaware on only one level

"No" she smiles from her bed
"just be here" she smiles

FIREBEARER

The fire was forged in the first haggard mountain that hefted it,
smouldering, from the folded core of the earth, bouldered
the scorched orb in its belly to be carried away, piece by piece,
on wicker torches that held its heat, just long enough to be passed,
light its time then change hands, on to the next assigned soul
who trudged, braced his back, blackened his nail beds, burnt his hands,
singed his earlobes, but refused to drop it.

In this way, it went on till it became old fashioned, bad hat,
uncool for a man to stand in the center square, hoist the tattered flames
above his head, and speak words that weren't his own
dressed in his tone for the current era. No –
It stank. Was too sure,
too simple, dredged up some ancient clockwork the world had long
forgotten, didn't care for, figured was no fun.

Yet it burns on, a spark
in the gut of the mountain, the eye of the woman behind the counter.

GABRIELA ANDREEVSKA, GREECE-MACEDONIA BORDER

People watch from their homes, but I cannot watch
I must go out

30 to 50 a day, one hundred, three hundred,
500 to a thousand refugees a day now
along the train tracks, waiting for buses
but they don't know they will need papers
to formalize a taxi in Serbia

Ten kilo-meters on foot?
Yes, I say – I draw a diagram
Don't walk on the tracks, walk beside
with your children

I bring everyday bags of food
Everybody is a person who needs somebody to talk to
I like to help because
It gives my life meaning

Can I take your photo for memory? Under this tent.

Syria? Yes. Afghanistan? Yes.
Iraq and Turkey? Yes, yes. On a raft.
Not good. Too much cold.
A baby drowned

We will never go back
    of course
We will go back to our homes

I give mostly bread and water and granola bars
juice and bananas.

I carry everything in these plastic bags.

ACCELERATED MOTION

People laid out across the planet, exhausted.
The appearance of flu, yet no flu.
A cough with no cold, a headache
disguised as meningitis.

A man wakes in Texas stiff in the neck
unable to look to the side for no reason at all.
A boy in Kigali wants to stare, bare-eyed, into the sun
or he hasn't the energy to curl his legs.

In Marseilles they vomit streaks of density
into bins and buckets. Tokyo, broken ankles,
to keep the people in place while they upgrade.

Grise Fiord – below freezing –
history lifts off scalding foreheads.
A single, congealed fog rising from crust
and core.

War is shed on continents in sections
of flaked skin. Fear disintegrates
in gargled salt. A toothache is a correction.
An eye infection: Grace in-veined.

The world over they're starving for root vegetables,
vitamin D, and H2O to make the connections.
More than anything, they need to sleep.

What is it? What is it? What is it? What is it?
they wonder, as the lights coalesce in secret
in their snoring cells.

Tomorrow, when everyone wakes, they will be brilliant
they'll be moving so fast they'll feel *Yes Yes Yes*
it has finally happened, we are finally here.

In every city, toddlers dance in sequenced spirals
around their fevered mothers, laughing
that they were born at such the right time.

INDEPENDENCE DAY

It was the day the flags came down,
unmasted. People wrote poems
in their passports, or coastered them
onto bartops and laid a pint down.
They lined the streets
to return their birth certificates.
Dropped their names into the mile-
wide horse's bucket at the citycentre.
Cleaned their toenails
with the corners of their credit cards.

They travelled in flocks to the creek silently
broadening its banks under the city.
And when asked, *What do you do?*
They said, *We live*.

TRUIMPHANT SUCCESS

Her rusted sword came up from below,
two-sided, rending the earth at their feet

followed by hands, and so on
inching out of the cleft soil

an elbow, a star-field eye,
a split chin, returning upward

She rose, patting the dirt from her trousers
a bloodied fist to the back to re-set the torso

and smiled: *My Children*
you are forgiven

Her open arms let loose an infinite beginning
And so, the world returned to The Mother

TODD BACHMAN, LORAIN COUNTY, OHIO

I'm no good at poetry, jesus, just a simple man
who wanted to do an un-selfish thing for somebody,
Mr. Credonsky, who helped raise my daughter.

So why shouldn't he walk her down the aisle with me
as her step-father? I'm not sayin' it was easy these 14 years
– hell, no – but family's are what you make 'em.

So I took 'im by the hand down the aisle
as a gesture, and there wasn't a dry eye in the house,
his-self included. My-self included.

No one knew I was gonna do it, his-self included,
my daughter included. She cried more than anybody
'cept her mother.

"It was the most impactful moment of my life," he said,
Mr. Credonsky. I'm draggin' 'im, all shocked, knees bucklin',
and go figure thousands of people commented on the photo

on the Internet. All over the friggin' world, 'cause we all know the truth
when we see it, and we see it far too infrequent, I gather,
if this stands out so easy as such a nice thing to do.

THE GALACTIC TEAM & THE DISSOLUTION OF KARMA

You and I were bound to destroy each other
for positive gains.

You and I were never going to function, nonetheless,
it would have been impossible not to give it a go.

You brought me down with you, and stayed
so I could rise back up.

    *

You were always going to be my sister, saddling the bad luck
so I could go on and invite you forward.

You registered, whole-heartedly, as my mother
and had some difficulty when I wouldn't listen, by design

You were madly in love with me, and came as my cousin
so I could remember the night of our own wedding.

    *

He was my son in another body
that I recognized at sixteen years.

He took the diabetes and agreed to the kidney failure
so the rest of us could remain nimble.

She sat at the head of the college classroom and loved me
because that is all we had ever known of each other.

    *

He came as a protector, and I knew
from the way he handled the motorcycle at 100mph.

He came as a protector, and I knew
from the white book of poetry left on the dresser.

She came as a protector, and I knew
because she worried, and gave of herself endlessly.

    *

He came as a right-handed warrior
and dropped to a knee at my feet.

He came as a right-handed warrior
and was ticked when there was nothing to battle.

He came as a right-handed warrior and wanted everyone
in uniforms.

He came as a right-handed warrior and knew
as soon as I did.

    *

He came as a helper, and I realized from the questions
he asked that I couldn't yet answer.

He came as a helper, and I realized because he prostrated himself
to Jesus Christ and was confused when the Book didn't make sense

He came as a helper, which is why we ended up
in the same dormitory.

*

She was a guardian, and the evidence was all in
the text messages.

She was a guardian, and the evidence was all in
the stocking full of gifts.

She was a guardian, and the evidence
was in the look on her face.

*

She was a lover, again and again
so I knew it was all possible.

She was a lover
and I saw us in rocking chairs.

She was a lover, who knew
there was someone else for me.

*

They came as friends, and I knew
because we laughed.

They came as friends, and I knew
because I wasn't alone.

They came as friends, and I knew
because I wanted to live again.

They came as friends, and I knew
because I felt no tension of contract.

*

He came as a reminder, through the vibrations
in his chest.

He came as a joy, through the vibrations
in his chest.

He came as a partner, through the vibrations
in his chest.

*

She came as a purifier, and sat by his head
like a sphynx.

She came as a purifier, so I knew
he was in soft hands.

He came as God in a turtle tank
extending his neck for pellets.

*

She came for reconciliation, and that is why
she was my roommate.

She came for reconciliation, so it's no wonder
she wanted to hug, and hug.

She came for reconciliation, and it was so apparent
because she couldn't forgive herself.

    *

She was a healer, and the frazzled sweater
didn't fool me.

She was a healer, and the pain was self-
inflicted.

She was a healer who damaged her own person
to demonstrate the procedure for return.

    *

She was an activator who signed up for trips around the world
though she had no money.

She was an activator who rang the bowls
under the eclipse.

She was an activator who stepped in a hole
on the side of a pyramid.

    *

She came as a leader, and got everyone else
on board first.

She came as a leader
and looked me in the eye.

She came as a leader and spoke to me
through the radio.

She came as a leader and held my hand
to draw me back to Atlantis.

*****

They were the sun,
and that is who I was waiting for.

They were the sun, and when we stood face to face
I knew who I was.

They were the sun, and when we touched
it was so clear to me why everyone else was here.

They were the sun, and when they remembered,
contracts dissolved and all that remained

was freedom.

MULTI-DIMENSIONAL

It's not so easy sometimes
to occupy
more than one dimension.

One foot is leaden
sucked in six feet of sledge
at the center of Europe's historic bloody heart,
charcoaled at the edges
from centuries of occupation
of distant lands, lands
I can call them down like rain
to my fingertips
and push them around the crystal sky
constructing cloud formations of castles
and people, joyous people
light as the inside of a balloon
bobbing over the pristine grasses
their returned lands,
lands slick with arterial fluid spilled
and marched on by millions,
lands like diamonds, a grounded
constellation leading home,
home-wrecked family's stretched and split, grieving
for home, home
hand in hand around a blazing, contented campfire
on an autumn evening
campfire, red fire, blue fire
Fire: taking
Fire: burning
Fire

releasing the clasped anguish of the earth
and all its aching bodies
in a single, momentous smoke.

Smoke, smoke a cigarette
with my feet up on the thunder mountains
watching our utopia flicker in and out.

LIGHTHEARTED

Detached from my chest
at the ventricles.
Floated past the eavestroughs,
spattering rooftops
and hitched a cloud.

Rode off yonder, laughing
at all the misplaced
seriousness
below.

REJOICE IN CELEBRATION

The Master stands on her parapet
appreciating globalization

for the way it brought us together
under a single consciousness.

Who knew, the system constructed
to keep us contained

would be the same
that un-did the false horse of fear

and connected us as Seven Billion
dazzling veins in a single organism.

A bright, beautiful beating heart
the size of a planet

in synch
one pulse.

∞

It was all timing
and it was time

with the infrastructure in place
internal and external pathways

leading to heaven
on earth.

∞

Who knew, the codes would pass through geometric
YouTube representations

and sun spots in music videos
in a way

that didn't work on Sinai's tablet
and failed in misery when the city sank.

Who knew, the energy could move over mountains
in jumbo jets

through eyes and wires
physical embrace

and voice patterns over blog radio.

Up through the soil and waterways
hidden in books, even the bestsellers

and the Hollywood hits enclosed
the message, once accepted

it all moved so quickly after eons

of patient agony.

∞

It was all timing
and it was time.

Who knew, the mass media would fall
to the naysayers on FaceBook.

Universal Tweets of awakening.
Who knew,

the conspiracy theorists had theorized correctly
and the truth tellers were really the palm readers

the star gazers and storm chasers
in their trucks with solar panels and greens on the roof.

Who knew, the banks would burn
without a fire   ,

the cops would retire their arms
simply because there was no work.

Who knew, the towers of terror weren't real
but the crop circles were

not to mention the visitations
the clandestine guidance, the meticulous ordering of the planets

the pyramids, and the stones with faces
and ten-foot bodies buried in the dirt.

Who knew, the heroes were the ones you staked
in heat

and celled in asylums
cemented

so many times, so many lifetimes

because they saw what others did not.
They knew.

∞

Who knew, the way it was foretold
was not the way it unfolded

so seamlessly, without violence
with such discretion (imperceptible apocalypse) because

a blossom has done much secret toiling
before it opens itself

to the Sun
which has been waiting in the same place

forever

for us to say: *Okay.*
We are ready. Here we are.

∞

It was all timing,
and it is time to rejoice in celebration:

The Master raises a jeweled cup over the land she loves
but does not own

it is yours again
and belongs to no-one.

ABOUT THE AUTHOR

Andrea Perry graduated from the Royal Military College of Canada in 2008 with a BA in English Literature and a Minor in Political Science. She served five years as an Intelligence Officer in the Canadian Army before releasing in 2013 to pursue a life-times long, multi-dimensional love of reading and writing. She has since completed an MFA in Creative Writing at the University of Guelph and now drifts between hometown Ottawa, new-town Guelph, and other travels. She writes poetry and fiction.

www.ingramcontent.com/pod-product-compliance
Lightning Source LLC
LaVergne TN
LVHW091314080426
835510LV00007B/498